I CHING OF THE STOCK MARKET

I CHING OF THE STOCK MARKET

MikeNach

DISCLAIMER

The author and publisher have used their best efforts in preparing this book. The author and publisher make no representation or warranties with respect to the accuracy, applicability or completeness of the contents of this book. If you wish to apply the ideas contained in this book, you are taking full responsibility for your action.

Every effort has been made to accurately represent the techniques mentioned in this book and their potential. However, there is no guarantee that you will succeed in any way using the techniques and ideas in this book. Your level of success in attaining the results claimed in this book depends on your mental makeup/ belief system, knowledge and the time you devote to the ideas and techniques mentioned. Since these factors differ according to individuals, we cannot guarantee your success; in fact no guarantees are made that you will achieve any results from the techniques and ideas in this book. Nor are we responsible for any of your actions. Consulting a competent professional is advisable.

The author and publisher shall in no event be held liable to any party for any direct, indirect, punitive, special, incidental or other consequential damages arising directly or indirectly from any use of this material, which is provided "as is", and without warranties.

The author and publisher do not warrant the performance, effectiveness or accountability of any sites listed or linked to this book. All links are for information purposes only and are not warranted for content, accuracy or any other implied or explicit purpose.

U.S Government Required Disclaimer: Forex, Futures, Stocks and Options trading are not appropriate for everyone. There is a substantial risk of loss associated with trading these markets. Losses can and will occur. No system or methodology has ever been developed that can guarantee profits or ensure freedom from losses.

Hypothetical or simulated results have certain limitations unlike an actual performance record. Simulated results do not represent actual trading also. Since the trades have not been executed, the results may have under-or-over compensated for the impact, if any, of certain market factors, such as lack of liquidity or unforeseen circumstances.

No representation or implication is being made that the techniques/systems mentioned in this book will generate profits or ensure freedom from losses.

Contents

WHEN IN DOUBT, CONSULT THE I CHING!

"If I have seen farther, it is by standing on the shoulder of giants."

— Sir Isaac Newton

Your phone rings. It's your stock broker on the line. He sounds excited.

"Hey, (your name)! I've this awesome stock for you. Buy it. It's going to be a multibagger before you know it."

What are you going to do about it? Act upon your broker's hype? If you have profited from your broker's calls in the past, then, I bet, you are going to grab his offer. And my story ends here.

But, if you are not sure about your broker's exhortations, then you will need to do the homework by checking out the company's financials (fundamental analysis) and its price action (technical analysis), before taking any action.

After doing the spadework, you (your conscious mind) figures out that your broker's got something there. The company is on a roll. Its stock price is also moving upwards. Everything about the company and it's stock smells good! An offer too good to refuse!

"Wowee! I'm going to be a millionaire!"

You can't wait to call your broker and place the order. Just then, your inner voice (your subconscious mind) whispers, "Wait! Don't believe that guy. He's taking you for a ride.The company's results are window dressing. The stock price will soon plunge."

Whoa! What now? Whose advice are you going to act upon?

Your broker's? Your inner voice?

You have two choices. **Buy the stock or leave it alone.**

What if your broker is right? You will surely profit if you buy the stock.You know, hunches can go wrong, sometimes!

Suppose your inner voice has guessed the situation correctly? You will end up cursing your broker for the huge loss staring at you.

How do you figure out what action to take?

If you are faced with a similar situation, then you need to consult the I Ching.

The I Ching is one of the oldest divination systems in the world. It has been in existence for thousands of years and millions of people over the ages, from emperors to commoners, have used it and greatly benefited from its advice. You will, too. Consulting the I Ching is like having, by your side, a wise and all-knowing personality that is always ready to help and advice whenever you need it. The very fact, that it's still popular today means that it has something going for it.

The stock market is a place where the information is not always dependable. Often, there's no correlation between the company's performance and its stock price. Rumors and false information abound the market. An inexperienced participant can easily make huge losses in such a situation. This makes investing / trading a very scary operation. It is no wonder that most people stay away from the market!

You need to have an edge if you want to make money in the stock market. If you don't have an edge, all the discipline and money management skills in this world will be of no use. You will lose badly. The I Ching will give you the required edge. It will advice you when or what to invest / trade or when to enter / stay out of the market. Sometimes you will not agree with the advice given. In retrospect, you will find the advice received was very appropriate for the prevailing circumstances.

This book is for the novice as well as the most experienced investor / trader. It will be your lifelong friend, prognosticator and guide.

Never be over confident when trading. It is not possible to win 100 percent of the time even with the best trading method. Our emotional state plays a great role in our success or failure in the stock market. The difference between great investors / traders and the ordinary is their ability to remain calm and isolated irrespective of what the markets are doing.

There may be times when you are stressed or just don't feel like trading. Then, don't! You might not receive correct information if your mind is disturbed. There is a possibility of making serious losses. You will lose faith in the system. It is essential to be in the right state of mind before you trade.

Hey! Never force a trade and **don't use the I Ching as a standalone trading method to decide the trades for you.** Never base your trading decisions on any single trading indicator. Do your preliminary homework. You need to study the companies fundamentals as well as the various technical price signals before you figure out whether to buy, sell, hold or leave a stock.

What's your take on a particular stock?

Do you have any lingering doubts about your analysis?

Use the I Ching for a final say in the matter. Then it's upto you whether you follow the advice or not.
Happy investing / trading!

THE PRINCIPLES OF THE I CHING

What is the I Ching?

The **I Ching, the Chinese Book of Change**, is an ancient and venerable book of divination. Its origins lie with Fu Hsi who ruled China before the flood (c. 3000 B.C.). The basic text was written by King Wen (1123 B.C.) and his son Duke Chou. The commentaries were written by Confucius (561-479 B.C.) and his followers.

The I Ching is a book of wisdom that makes "Change" the center of observation and identifies time as an important factor in the world's structure and human development. The stock market also depends on price changes with time. Based on the market participant's interpretation of the various situations affecting the listed companies, the stock prices keep on fluctuating during the entire trading period. The stock market discounts all available information and this is reflected in the stock prices. This may be true only for the information known at the time.

What if this information is not fully understood by the market participants?

What about information that is yet to originate (state of potentiality)?

If you are new to the workings of the I Ching, you might be **skeptical** as to how the patterns formed by placing of six COIN / CANDLEs in a particular order can determine the outcome of the stock market. The I Ching is based upon the theory of **synchronicity**. When you ask the guidance of the I Ching, your placing of the six COIN / CANDLEs produces a unique pattern whose interpretations synchronizes with the market situation at that moment. This system has worked perfectly through the centuries and so there is no need for us to doubt its effectiveness.

Have faith and practice the timeless principles given in this book. Follow the trading advice and you will be richly rewarded for your efforts. Do not expect accurate results at the outset. It will take time for your subconscious mind to connect with the I Ching. Be patient. Learn how to place the COIN / CANDLEs and identify the pattern formed. Check the advice given against the actual market conditions. It is preferable that initially you paper trade so that you do not lose any money. After you become confident and proficient in this technique, start consulting the I Ching during actual trading situations.

USING I CHING TO CONNECT WITH THE MARKET

In th 2014 edition of this book, I told you how to use six coins to connect with your subconscious mind and figure out what the market will probably do in the future. In this edition, I will be using Price Action and Japanese candle sticks of any stock, ETF or index for divination of the market. So, here are the three methods:

I. USING THE SIX COINS FOR DIVINATION (2014 edition)

The **secret** of the world's greatest investors / traders has been their **intuition or 'gut feeling'**. Similarly, spectacular stock market losers have attributed their failures to the sudden desertion of their gut feeling or luck factor. Often, we mistake wishful thinking for intuition. If wishful thinking takes precedence over our gut feeling, then we are bound to make errors of judgment and suffer great losses.

Where does this gut feeling come from? **Your subconscious mind!** Everything in our universe is interconnected. The interrelated events may not be perceptible to us as they lie beyond our normal senses. The subconscious mind apparently is in tune with this universal consciousness. According to the ancients, there is a **'Universal Consciousness'** which pervades the entire empty space around us. This consciousness is the repository of all knowledge / information-past, present and future.

It is possible to access this information through our subconscious mind. However, due to background noise, it becomes difficult to single out the most suitable answer to a particular situation. The **I Ching** will help you connect. It will filter out the background noise. It will also warn you against wishful thinking.

The traditional I Ching comprises of **64 hexagrams** and each of these hexagrams contains six lines. Each line is either an unbroken (Yang) or a broken (Yin) line (totaling 384 line oracles altogether) and has a specific oracle attached to it. I have renamed the hexagrams as **'PATTERNS'** because the yang and yin lines have been replaced by '+' and '-' correspondingly, in my book. The reply to your question will be the oracle represented by the **'marked'** coin (see explanation below) in the pattern formed by the six coins.

SIX COINS: To work the six coins technique, you need six small coins of similar denomination. One of the coins need to be slightly different but easily distinguishable from the other five. I will call this coin as the 'marked' coin and its position, in the pattern generated, determines the answer to your question. After use, keep these coins in a safe place, as you will be using the same coins for future readings.

HOW TO USE THE SIX COINS?

1: Sit comfortably in a quiet room.

2: Maintain a diary to note your readings. Write the date, time and your stock query before you begin.

3: Cup the six coins in your two hands.

4: Think about your question. Be focused. Do not try to force favorable answers in your mind.

5: Take a few deep breaths. Empty your mind of extraneous thoughts. Relax.

6: Shake the coins, until your inner voice tells you that they are 'ready' to be placed.

7: Keep your eyes closed. You do not want to manipulate the results by looking at the coins.

8: Transfer the coins to one of your hands.

9: Use your other hand to pick the coins at random, and place them one after the other on the table.

10: Line up the coins in a vertical column, in the order in which they were picked, from bottom to top. Thus, the first coin will be nearest to you and the last coin farthest.

11: Note the side ('HEADS' up or 'TAILS' up) and the placement order of each coin. The Heads up will be denoted as "+" and the Tails up are "-."

12: Highlight the position of your marked coin in the pattern.

13: Consult the Pattern Lookup Table (see below) and find the upper half of your pattern on the top and the lower half on the left. Follow the column and row to where they meet. That will be your pattern number.

14: Go to the designated pattern and read the oracle for the line represented by the marked coin.

15: That's the answer to your question.

16: Example- In case the above description is not clear, the following example will help you understand. Check out the following coins arrangement-

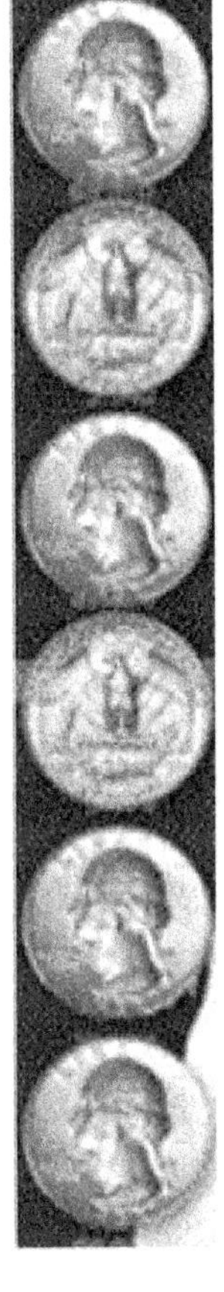

Sixth coin Heads (H)

Fifth coin Tails (T)

Fourth coin Heads (H)

Third coin [Marked] Tails (T)

Second coin Heads (H)

First coin Heads (H)

The six coins are arranged in a vertical column. They were placed in the order in which they were picked, from bottom to top, in the column. The first coin picked, showed 'Heads (+)' up. The second coin was 'Heads (+)' up. The third coin which was the marked coin was 'Tails

(-)' up. The fourth, fifth and sixth coins were 'Heads(+)', 'Tails (-)' and 'Heads (+)' correspondingly.

Now, locate the pattern number, for the above configuration, from the Pattern Lookup Table. It is pattern 38.

PATTERN 38: THE ESTRANGED

INTERPRETATION

6th COIN / CANDLE: +

After initial setback, the price of your stock will recover.

5th COIN / CANDLE: -

You will do well in this trade.

4th COIN / CANDLE: +

If your stock has been out of favor expect some favorable news soon.

3rd COIN / CANDLE: -

After initial setback, the price of your stock will recover.

2nd COIN / CANDLE: +

Your stock will trade in a narrow range.

1st COIN / CANDLE: +

Stay away from overpriced/ unknown/ under-performing or thinly traded stocks.

Now read the advice given for the marked COIN / CANDLE (3rd COIN / CANDLE).
The advice given is- **'After initial setback, the price of your stock will recover'.**

That's the advice to your stock query!

17: Asking questions- The proper way to ask a question is as follows-

"I am interested in buying/ selling/ trading stock (name?) at this price (specify correct amount). What will be the likely outcome if take action and hold on to this position for a period of --- (specify the time period)?"

Follow the advice received.

18: Not the right advice?- If you feel you have received an apparently contradictory reading for your query, it might mean that either you were not in a proper frame of mind or your question was not focused on a single stock. Was your question a double either / or type? If so, then you will not be able to decide which of the two questions were answered. Also, if you are skeptical about the six coins technique, be sure, you aren't going to get any correct answers. **Be respectful and BELIEVE!**

Do not try to force favorable answers from the oracle by consulting it more than once for the same stock, for the day. If you ask the same question, again and again, you will obtain different patterns with different guidance. This would be of no value to you. **Usually, the advice you receive on the first occasion is the most appropriate one.**

When you have received the best advice there is no need to seek further clarifications. You have three choices- act upon it **OR** ignore it **OR** consult the oracle about this stock, the next day.

19: There is no limit to the number of stocks you can consult the oracle in a day. Ensure that you are relaxed and focused before you consult the I Ching.

20: Hey! Remember **the one stock / one question rule**.

II. USING PRICE ACTION

There were a few readers of the first edition who were skeptical about using six coins to divine the market. They felt that such techniques don't make any sense. Okay, guys, I hear you guys. We will checkout Price Action and Japanese Candlesticks to divine the stock market just like professional traders.

Let's start by looking at seven consecutive closing prices starting with the most recent price down to the price seven days/periods back.

If you are a swing trader (holding a stock for 1 – 10 days), you will need to use seven consecutive daily closing prices to check out the market situation for the next day to a few days.

If you need to know what's the situation is going to be for the following week then you need to use seven consecutive weekly closing prices. Weekly charts are used by positional traders who hold a stock for more than a week to several months. Weekly Charts are generally used to identify yearly trends, growth trends etc.

Likewise for monthly charts. Monthly charts are used by intermediate or short-term traders who hold a stock for less than a year or for long term investors who wish to change their style from holding for many years to holding a few months or less than a year. Monthly charts are also used for Sector Analysis, and Industry Analysis.

Let's take an example to illustrate what I said above. Check out the dates and the close prices of a stock "X."

Date	Close	
March 11, 2021	699.6	+

March 10, 2021	668.06	-
March 9, 2021	673.58	**+**
March 8, 2021	563	-
March 5, 2021	597.95	-
March 4, 2021	621.44	-
March 3, 2021	653.2	

These are the seven consecutive daily close prices of a stock arranged in a descending order of dates. You will start with the close price of March11 which is 699.6. If you compare it with close price 668.06 of the previous day March 10, you observe that the close price of March 11 is higher than the close price of March 10. You will denote this as '+" in our third column. Let's check out whether the close price of March 10 is higher than the March 9 close price. It is not because 668.06 is lower than 673.58. You will denote this as "-" in our third column. Likewise do the same four more times to complete your stock's hexagram.

Now, locate the pattern number, for the above configuration, from the Pattern Lookup Table. It is pattern 35 (see below). These are the six possible outcomes for your stock which you need to bear in mind while trading in this stock.

PATTERN 35: PROGRESS

INTERPRETATION

6th COIN / CANDLE: +

This stock is probably influenced by high frequency traders.

5th COIN / CANDLE: -

Plan your entry/exit points for this trade. Use stop loss.

4th COIN / CANDLE: +

Limit your position in this stock. Have patience and you will be successful.

3rd COIN / CANDLE: -

You will do well in this trade.

2nd COIN / CANDLE: -

A stock tip from a reliable source might prove more profitable than your chosen stock.

1st COIN / CANDLE: -

If your stock is showing a definitive trend then take a position.

III. USING THE JAPANESE CANDLESTICKS FOR DIVINATION

Now, let's use the Japanese candlesticks to checkout what the market has in store for us. <u>This method works with the ordinary Japanese candlesticks only and not with Heikin Ashi candles, Hollow candles etc.</u>

If you are an investor or a trader I guess you know about Japanese candlesticks. So, I am not going to dive deep into candlesticks theory and will stick with the basics only.

A candlestick (see below figure) shows the market's open, high, low, and close price for the day. The candlestick has a wide part, which is called the "real body."

This real body represents the price range between the open and close of that day's trading. When the real body is empty or White / Green, it means the close was higher than the open. If the real body is filled in or Black / Red, it means the close was lower than the open. Sometimes when the open and close prices are same or very near to each other you are not gonna see the real body of the candle. In such cases, you need to check out the open and close prices to figure out whether it's a White / Green or a Black / Red candlestick.

Just above and below the real body are the "shadows" or "wicks." The shadows show the high and low prices of that day's trading. The relationship between the days open, high, low, and close determines the look of the daily candlestick. Real bodies can be long or short and black or white. Shadows can be long or short.

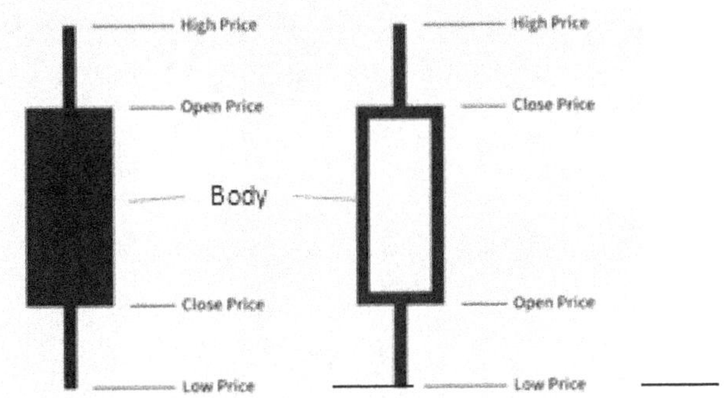

You will be using daily, weekly or monthly candlestick charts for your divination.

Each chart timeframe has a different purpose. You will follow the same method as you did in method II.

If you are a swing trader (holding a stock for 1 – 10 days), you will use daily charts to check out the market situation for the next day to a few days.

If you need to know what's the situation is going to be for the following week then you need to use weekly charts. Likewise for monthly charts.

What about the day trader?

I guess I Ching is not suitable for day trading charts. Sorry, guys!

How do we use the candlesticks to make our prediction?

Let's check out the six consecutive candlesticks of a stock starting with March 4 and ending with March 11.

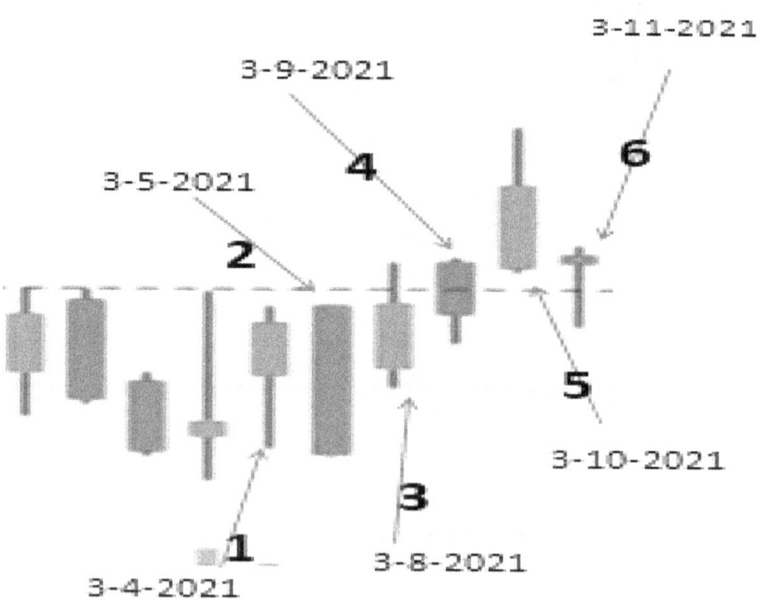

Date	Candle	
March 11, 2021	Red/ Black	-
March 10, 2021	Green/ White	+
March 9, 2021	Red/ Black	-
March 8, 2021	Green/ White	+
March 5, 2021	Red/ Black	-
March 4, 2021	Green/ White	+

The candle of March11 was Red/ Black which means the close price was lower than the open price. There were Red/ Black candles on March 9 and 5 accordingly. Likewise, there were Green/ White candles on March 10, 8 and 4. You will denote the Green/ White candles as "+" and Red/ Black candles as "-." Arrange the candles in the descending order of dates (as shown above) and checking out the Pattern Lookup Table, locate the pattern number, for the above configuration. It is pattern 63 (see below). These are the six possible outcomes for your stock which you need to bear in mind while trading in this stock.

PATTERN 63: AFTER COMPLETION

INTERPRETATION

6th COIN / CANDLE: -

After a severe initial setback, the price of your stock will recover.

5th COIN / CANDLE: +

Stocks of companies situated in the west will do well.

4th COIN / CANDLE: -

Expect mixed results with this stock.

3rd COIN / CANDLE: +

If the market is bearish then wait.

2nd COIN / CANDLE: -

Today's trade may turn profitable in a week's time.

1st COIN / CANDLE: +

You might be stopped out or you will exit in panic. Be patient. Have a contingency plan.

That's it guys. Please remember not to use the I Ching as a standalone indicator. It will give you advice but you need to do your homework as well.

Wishing you all the best with your trading!

PATTERN LOOKUP TABLE

→ ↓	+ + +	- - +	- + -	+ - -	- - -	+ + -	+ - +	- + +
+ + +	1	34	5	26	11	9	14	43
- - +	25	51	3	27	24	42	21	17
- + -	6	40	29	4	7	59	64	47
+ - -	33	62	39	52	15	53	56	31
- - -	12	16	8	23	2	20	35	45
+ + -	44	32	48	18	46	57	50	28
+ - +	13	55	63	22	36	37	30	49
- + +	10	54	60	41	19	61	38	58

H= +   **T= -**

Find the upper half of your pattern at the top ($\rightarrow$) and the lower half on the left ($\downarrow$) and follow the row and column to where they intersect. That will be the number of your pattern.

THE 64 PATTERNS AND THEIR LINEWISE INTERPRETATIONS

PATTERN 1: THE CREATIVE

INTERPRETATION

6th COIN / CANDLE: +

Expect a probable loss for this trade.

5th COIN / CANDLE: +

If the price of this stock is rising then consult your stock broker/advisor before implementation.

4th COIN / CANDLE: +

Limit your position in this stock. Use stop loss.

3rd COIN / CANDLE: +

Choose a better stock than this one.

2nd COIN / CANDLE: +

Ask the advice of your stock broker/ advisor before you trade this stock.

1st COIN / CANDLE: +

Wait for a better opportunity to present itself soon.

PATTERN 2: THE RECEPTIVE

INTERPRETATION

6th COIN / CANDLE: -

This stock will experience selling pressure.

5th COIN / CANDLE: -

You will do well in this trade.

4th COIN / CANDLE: -

This stock might exhibit price volatility. Plan your entry/ exit points, stop loss before you trade.

3rd COIN / CANDLE: -

After initial setback, the price of your stock will recover. If it is a relatively unknown stock then it will soon become newsworthy.

2nd COIN / CANDLE: -

You will do well in this trade.

1st COIN / CANDLE: -

Market conditions are going to change which will adversely affect your stock.

PATTERN 3: DIFFICULTY

INTERPRETATION

6th COIN / CANDLE: -

You will have to hold on this stock for a while.

5th COIN / CANDLE: +

Limit your initial position in this stock. Increase position after watching its price action.

4th COIN / CANDLE: -

You will do well in this trade.

3rd COIN / CANDLE: -

Expect a probable loss for this trade.

2nd COIN / CANDLE: -

You will have to hold on this stock for a while.

1st COIN / CANDLE: +

Wait for a better opportunity to present itself soon.

PATTERN 4: IMMATURITY

INTERPRETATION

6th COIN / CANDLE: +

If your chosen stock is of a newer company then please check its performance before investing/ trading. Otherwise, invest in a stable stock of an established company.

5th COIN / CANDLE: -

Your profit probabilities are higher with stocks of promising new companies.

4th COIN / CANDLE: -

Choose a better stock than this one.

3rd COIN / CANDLE: -

Don't invest/ trade in this stock if it had shown extreme price volatility in the past.

2nd COIN / CANDLE: +

Invest/ trade in this stock only if the market is bullish.

1st COIN / CANDLE: -

Don't expect much from this stock.

PATTERN 5: WAITING

INTERPRETATION

6th COIN / CANDLE: -

Trust your judgment on this stock.

5th COIN / CANDLE: +

Wait for the price of your stock/ the market to stabilize before entering your position.

4th COIN / CANDLE: -

Wait. Don't invest/ trade in this stock now.

3rd COIN / CANDLE: +

Wait. Don't invest/ trade in this stock now.

2nd COIN / CANDLE: +

There are lots of rumors and misinformation about this stock. Wait for prices to stabilize before investing/ trading.

1st COIN / CANDLE: +

Wait. Don't invest/ trade in this stock now.

PATTERN 6: CONFLICT

INTERPRETATION

6th COIN / CANDLE: +

Your stock will exhibit extreme price volatility. Exiting your position will be difficult.

5th COIN / CANDLE: +

After initial setback, the price of your stock will recover.

4th COIN / CANDLE: +

Wait. Don't invest/ trade in this stock now.

3rd COIN / CANDLE: -

After initial setback, the price of your stock will recover.

2nd COIN / CANDLE: +

If you indulge in contrarian investing/ trading for this stock, then you will lose.

1st COIN / CANDLE: -

This stock is a short term play. Plan your entry/exit points for this trade. Use stop loss.

PATTERN 7: THE ARMY

INTERPRETATION

6th COIN / CANDLE: -

If your stock is of a poorly performing company, its price will be affected.

5th COIN / CANDLE: -

Choose leading/ stable stocks if the market conditions are chaotic.

4th COIN / CANDLE: -

Wait for present conditions/ trend to change before taking a position.

3rd COIN / CANDLE: -

Expect a probable loss for this trade.

2nd COIN / CANDLE: +

Invest in leading stocks or stocks favored by insiders, institutions and analysts.

1st COIN / CANDLE: -

Limit your initial position in this stock. Increase your position steadily only after its price action is clear.

PATTERN 8: UNITY

INTERPRETATION

6th COIN / CANDLE: -

Wait. Don't invest/ trade in this stock now.

5th COIN / CANDLE: +

If your stock is showing a definitive trend then take a position.

4th COIN / CANDLE: -

Investing/ trading in stocks of companies favored by analysts and institutional investors will be profitable.

3rd COIN / CANDLE: -

If your stock is of a recently downgraded company, then you will have a loss.

2nd COIN / CANDLE: -

If your stock is an unknown, under-performing or thinly traded stock then don't take a position.

1st COIN / CANDLE: -

There is a high probability of unexpected profits from this trade.

PATTERN 9: THE RESTRAINING

INTERPRETATION

6th COIN / CANDLE: +

You will have to hold on this stock for a long period since there is a possibility of price reversal.

5th COIN / CANDLE: +

Your profit probabilities are higher with leading stocks/ market favorites.

4th COIN / CANDLE: -

If you are willing to accept a certain level of risk, then take a position. Be prepared for small profits.

3rd COIN / CANDLE: +

Wait. Market conditions are very choppy.

2nd COIN / CANDLE: +

Going short on this stock has more profit possibilities.

1st COIN / CANDLE: +

You will do well in this trade.

PATTERN 10: TREADING

INTERPRETATION

6th COIN / CANDLE: +

Plan your entry/exit points for this trade. Use stop loss. Stay with the trend.

5th COIN / CANDLE: +

Wait. Don't invest/ trade in this stock now.

4th COIN / CANDLE: +

After initial setback, the price of your stock will recover.

3rd COIN / CANDLE: -

Don't over leverage your position in this stock. Limit your position.

2nd COIN / CANDLE: +

Trade in leading stocks of fundamentally strong companies for the long term.

1st COIN / CANDLE: +

Invest/ trade in small lots. Use stop loss.

PATTERN 11: PEACE

INTERPRETATION

6ᵗʰ COIN / CANDLE: -
Expect a probable loss for this trade.

5ᵗʰ COIN / CANDLE: -
Invest in fundamentally strong companies or companies which have undergone consolidation..

4ᵗʰ COIN / CANDLE: -
Don't trade on tips and rumors.

3ʳᵈ COIN / CANDLE: +
Expect mixed results with this stock.

2ⁿᵈ COIN / CANDLE: +
You will have to hold on this stock for a while. There is a possibility of small profits.

1ˢᵗ COIN / CANDLE: +
There is a probability of receiving additional benefits from this stock, like dividends, stock-splits, buyouts…….., if you hold on to your position.

PATTERN 12: STAGNATION

INTERPRETATION

6th COIN / CANDLE: +

If your stock is showing a definitive trend then take a position.

5th COIN / CANDLE: +

This stock might sit, where it is now, for a long period or exhibit sudden price reversal.

4th COIN / CANDLE: +

Investing/ trading in stocks of companies favored by analysts and institutional investors will be profitable.

3rd COIN / CANDLE: -

Expect a probable loss for this trade.

2nd COIN / CANDLE: -

If your stock is showing a definitive trend then take a position for a short period. Expect a price reversal very soon.

1st COIN / CANDLE: -

There is a probability of receiving additional benefits from this stock like dividends, stock-splits, buyouts…..., if you hold on to your position.

PATTERN 13: FELLOWSHIP

INTERPRETATION

6th COIN / CANDLE: +
You will have to hold on this stock for a while.

5th COIN / CANDLE: +
After initial setback, the price of your stock will recover.

4th COIN / CANDLE: +
Wait for a better opportunity to present itself soon.

3rd COIN / CANDLE: +
You will have to hold on this stock for a while.

2nd COIN / CANDLE: -
Expect a probable loss for this trade.

1st COIN / CANDLE: +
Choose a stock which is the current market favorite.

PATTERN 14: GREAT POSSESION

INTERPRETATION

6th COIN / CANDLE: +
You will do well in this trade.

5th COIN / CANDLE: -
You will do well in this trade.

4th COIN / CANDLE: +
You will do well in this trade.

3rd COIN / CANDLE: +
Don't trade in institutional stocks.

2nd COIN / CANDLE: +
Plan your entry/exit points for this trade. Use stop loss. There is a possibility of price reversal.

1st COIN / CANDLE: +
Wait. Don't invest/ trade in this stock now.

PATTERN 15: MODESTY

INTERPRETATION

6th COIN / CANDLE: -

If your stock is showing a definitive trend then take a position.

5th COIN / CANDLE: -

Limit your position in this stock. Have patience and you will be successful.

4th COIN / CANDLE: -

Limit your position in this stock. Have patience and you will be successful.

3rd COIN / CANDLE: +

Limit your position in this stock. Have patience and you will be successful.

2nd COIN / CANDLE: -

Limit your position in this stock. Have patience and you will be successful.

1st COIN / CANDLE: -

You will do very well in this trade.

PATTERN 16: REPOSE

INTERPRETATION

6th COIN / CANDLE: -

If your stock is showing a definitive trend then take a position.

5th COIN / CANDLE: -

After initial setback, the price of your stock will recover.

4th COIN / CANDLE: +

You will do well in this trade.

3rd COIN / CANDLE: -

Plan your entry/exit points for this trade. Use stop loss. There is a possibility of price reversal.

2nd COIN / CANDLE: -

There is a possibility of your position turning profitable at the end of the trading period.

1st COIN / CANDLE: -

Expect a probable loss for this trade.

PATTERN 17: FOLLOWING

INTERPRETATION

6th COIN / CANDLE: -
Choose a better stock than this one.

5th COIN / CANDLE: +
You will do well in this trade.

4th COIN / CANDLE: +
Expect a probable loss if you let your emotions influence this trade.

3rd COIN / CANDLE: -
Choose a better stock than this one.

2nd COIN / CANDLE: -
Choose a better stock than this one.

1st COIN / CANDLE: +
Choose a stock which is the current market favorite.

PATTERN 18: DECAY

INTERPRETATION

6ᵗʰ COIN / CANDLE: +
Don't trade in public sector stocks or stocks which depend upon government contracts.

5ᵗʰ COIN / CANDLE: -
There are profit possibilities in stocks of companies which have restructured or made changes in its top management.

4ᵗʰ COIN / CANDLE: -
There are profit possibilities in stocks of companies which have restructured or made changes in its top management.

3ʳᵈ COIN / CANDLE: +
There are profit possibilities in stocks of companies which have restructured or made changes in its top management.

2ⁿᵈ COIN / CANDLE: +
Stay away, if the price of this stock is falling, thinly traded, or the company is facing management problems.

1ˢᵗ COIN / CANDLE: -

There are profit possibilities in stocks of companies which have restructured or made changes in its top management.

PATTERN 19: APPROACH

INTERPRETATION

6th COIN / CANDLE: -
You will do well in this trade.

5th COIN / CANDLE: -
You will do well in this trade.

4th COIN / CANDLE: -
You will do well in this trade.

3rd COIN / CANDLE: -
Expect a probable loss from this trade.

2nd COIN / CANDLE: +
This stock might have sudden price swings. Plan your entry/exit points for this trade. Use stop loss.

1st COIN / CANDLE: +
You will do well in this trade.

PATTERN 20: CONTEMPLATION

INTERPRETATION

6th COIN / CANDLE: +

Expect a probable loss if you let your emotions influence this trade.

5th COIN / CANDLE: +

Choose a market favorite stock for short term trade.

4th COIN / CANDLE: -

Choose a better stock than this one.

3rd COIN / CANDLE: -

Expect a probable loss if you let your emotions influence this trade.

2nd COIN / CANDLE: -

This stock will trade in a narrow range. Plan your entry/exit points for this trade. Use stop loss.

1st COIN / CANDLE: -

Profits, if any, will not be as per your expectation.

PATTERN 21: BITING THROUGH

INTERPRETATION

6th COIN / CANDLE: +

Expect a probable loss for this trade.

5th COIN / CANDLE: -

Choose a better stock than this one.

4th COIN / CANDLE: +

After initial setback, the price of your stock will recover.

3rd COIN / CANDLE: -

Stay away, if the price of this stock is falling or if it is thinly traded.

2nd COIN / CANDLE: -

This stock is probably influenced by high frequency traders.

1st COIN / CANDLE: +

This stock is probably influenced by high frequency traders.

PATTERN 22: ELEGANCE

INTERPRETATION

6th COIN / CANDLE: +
You will do well in this trade.

5th COIN / CANDLE: -
After initial setback, the price of your stock will recover.

4th COIN / CANDLE: -
Don't expect much from this stock.

3rd COIN / CANDLE: +
You will do well in this trade.

2nd COIN / CANDLE: -
If this stock is an impulsive pick then watch out for false moves.

1st COIN / CANDLE: +
Trust your judgment. Don't follow others advice.

PATTERN 23: PEELING OFF

INTERPRETATION

6th COIN / CANDLE: +
You will do well in this trade.

5th COIN / CANDLE: -
You will do well in this trade.

4th COIN / CANDLE: -
Expect a probable loss for this trade.

3rd COIN / CANDLE: -
Expect a probable loss for this trade.

2nd COIN / CANDLE: -
Expect a probable loss for this trade.

1st COIN / CANDLE: -
Expect a probable loss for this trade.

PATTERN 24: RETURN

INTERPRETATION

6th COIN / CANDLE: -

Expect a probable loss for this trade.

5th COIN / CANDLE: -

Expect mixed results with this stock. You will have to be vigilant.

4th COIN / CANDLE: -

This stock will have few takers when you want to exit.

3rd COIN / CANDLE: -

If you trade in this stock, you can expect see-saw price action afterwards.

2nd COIN / CANDLE: -

You will do well in this trade.

1st COIN / CANDLE: +

Exit as soon as your trade is profitable.

PATTERN 25: CIRCUMSPECTION

INTERPRETATION

6ᵗʰ COIN / CANDLE: +

Choose a better stock than this one.

5ᵗʰ COIN / CANDLE: +

Profits, if any, will not be as per your expectation.

4ᵗʰ COIN / CANDLE: +

Don't anticipate huge gains. Exit as soon as your trade is profitable.

3ʳᵈ COIN / CANDLE: -

There is a probability of a sudden price reversal after you take a position in this stock.

2ⁿᵈ COIN / CANDLE: -

Don't anticipate huge gains. Exit as soon as your trade is profitable.

1ˢᵗ COIN / CANDLE: +

You will do well in this trade.

PATTERN 26: THE GREAT NOURISHER

INTERPRETATION

6th COIN / CANDLE: +

You will do well in this trade.

5th COIN / CANDLE: -

You will do well in this trade.

4th COIN / CANDLE: -

You will do well in this trade.

3rd COIN / CANDLE: +

Successful trade if you set a target price to exit.

2nd COIN / CANDLE: +

Stay away, if this stock is thinly traded or its price is falling.

1st COIN / CANDLE: +

Exit from any open position.

PATTERN 27: NOURISHMENT

INTERPRETATION

6th COIN / CANDLE: +

Expect mixed results with this stock.

5th COIN / CANDLE: -

Trade in high probability stocks. Leave volatile stocks alone.

4th COIN / CANDLE: -

You will do well in this trade.

3rd COIN / CANDLE: -

You will have to hold on this stock for a while.

2nd COIN / CANDLE: -

Don't try a new/ unfamiliar trading strategy or invest/ trade in unknown stocks.

1st COIN / CANDLE: +

Expect a probable loss if you let your emotions influence this trade.

PATTERN 28: EXCESS

INTERPRETATION

6th COIN / CANDLE: -
Expect a probable loss for this trade.

5th COIN / CANDLE: +
Don't trade if your stock is a merger/ acquisition play or downgraded by analysts.

4th COIN / CANDLE: +
Your trade will be successful if you exit when it is showing a profit.

3rd COIN / CANDLE: +
This stock will have few takers when you want to exit.

2nd COIN / CANDLE: +
Take a position in the stock of a company which has recently acquired a new promising company.

1st COIN / CANDLE: -
Your profit probabilities are higher with stocks showing steady price action.

PATTERN 29: THE ABYSS

INTERPRETATION

6th COIN / CANDLE: -
If the market is bearish then wait.

5th COIN / CANDLE: +
Wait for the market to stabilize before taking a position.

4th COIN / CANDLE: -
You will have to hold on this stock for a while.

3rd COIN / CANDLE: -
Expect a probable loss for this trade.

2nd COIN / CANDLE: +
Don't expect much from this stock.

1st COIN / CANDLE: -
Expect a probable loss for this trade.

PATTERN 30: FLAMING BEAUTY

INTERPRETATION

6th COIN / CANDLE: +
Wait. The market's in a consolidation phase.

5th COIN / CANDLE: -
Trade in index stocks or stocks favored by institutions.

4th COIN / CANDLE: +
You will have to exit quickly to make a profit.

3rd COIN / CANDLE: +
You will have to exit quickly to make a profit.

2nd COIN / CANDLE: -
You will do well in this trade.

1st COIN / CANDLE: +
Limit your position in this stock. Have patience and you will be successful.

PATTERN 31: STIMULATION

INTERPRETATION

6th COIN / CANDLE: -
Wait for volatile conditions to subside before taking a position.

5th COIN / CANDLE: +
Wait for volatile conditions to subside before taking a position.

4th COIN / CANDLE: +
You will do well in this trade.

3rd COIN / CANDLE: +
Wait for a better opportunity to present itself soon.

2nd COIN / CANDLE: -
Wait for a better opportunity to present itself soon.

1st COIN / CANDLE: -
Expect mixed results with this stock.

PATTERN 32: CONTINUITY

INTERPRETATION

6th COIN / CANDLE: -

Wait for volatile conditions to subside before taking a position.

5th COIN / CANDLE: -

Your profit probabilities are higher with stocks of medium size companies.

4th COIN / CANDLE: +

If you are willing to take a risk then go ahead.

3rd COIN / CANDLE: +

Expect a probable loss for this trade.

2nd COIN / CANDLE: +

Don't over leverage your position in this stock. Limit your position.

1st COIN / CANDLE: -

Don't try to force this trade. This stock will not deliver a quick profit.

PATTERN 33: RETREAT

INTERPRETATION

6th COIN / CANDLE: +

Wait for volatile conditions to subside before taking a position.

5th COIN / CANDLE: +

Wait for volatile conditions to subside before taking a position.

4th COIN / CANDLE: +

Wait for volatile conditions to subside before taking a position.

3rd COIN / CANDLE: +

Expect mixed results with this stock.

2nd COIN / CANDLE: -

Your stock will be trading in a narrow range.

1st COIN / CANDLE: -

Expect mixed results with this stock.

PATTERN 34: THE POWER OF THE GREAT

INTERPRETATION

6th COIN / CANDLE: -

After initial setback, the price of your stock will recover.

5th COIN / CANDLE: -

Don't try to force this trade. This stock will not deliver a quick profit.

4th COIN / CANDLE: +

You will do well in this trade.

3rd COIN / CANDLE: +

Don't try to force this trade. This stock will not deliver a quick profit.

2nd COIN / CANDLE: +

You will do well in this trade.

1st COIN / CANDLE: +

Expect a probable loss for this trade.

PATTERN 35: PROGRESS

INTERPRETATION

6th COIN / CANDLE: +

This stock is probably influenced by high frequency traders.

5th COIN / CANDLE: -

Plan your entry/exit points for this trade. Use stop loss.

4th COIN / CANDLE: +

Limit your position in this stock. Have patience and you will be successful.

3rd COIN / CANDLE: -

You will do well in this trade.

2nd COIN / CANDLE: -

A stock tip from a reliable source might prove more profitable than your chosen stock.

1st COIN / CANDLE: -

If your stock is showing a definitive trend then take a position.

PATTERN 36: DARKENING OF LIGHT

INTERPRETATION

6th COIN / CANDLE: -

This stock will soon reach price exhaustion and start falling.

5th COIN / CANDLE: -

You will do well in this trade with proper money management.

4th COIN / CANDLE: -

Choose a better stock than this one.

3rd COIN / CANDLE: +

Don't over leverage your position in this stock. Limit your position.

2nd COIN / CANDLE: -

If your stock is showing a definitive trend then take a position.

1st COIN / CANDLE: +

You will have to hold on this stock for a while.

PATTERN 37: THE FAMILY

INTERPRETATION

6th COIN / CANDLE: +

Your profit probabilities are higher with leading stocks.

5th COIN / CANDLE: +

Your profit probabilities are higher with leading stocks.

4th COIN / CANDLE: -

You will do well in this trade.

3rd COIN / CANDLE: +

Be wary if your stock has been downgraded by analysts or is subject of rumors.

2nd COIN / CANDLE: -

Your profit probabilities are higher with conservative stocks.

1st COIN / CANDLE: +

Your profit probabilities are higher with conservative stocks.

PATTERN 38: THE ESTRANGED

INTERPRETATION

6th COIN / CANDLE: +
After initial setback, the price of your stock will recover.

5th COIN / CANDLE: -
You will do well in this trade.

4th COIN / CANDLE: +
If your stock has been out of favor expect some favorable news soon.

3rd COIN / CANDLE: -
After initial setback, the price of your stock will recover.

2nd COIN / CANDLE: +
Your stock will trade in a narrow range.

1st COIN / CANDLE: +
Stay away from overpriced/ unknown/ under-performing or thinly traded stocks.

PATTERN 39: OBSTRUCTION

INTERPRETATION

6th COIN / CANDLE: -
Ask the advice of your stock broker / advisor before you trade this stock.

5th COIN / CANDLE: +
Wait for volatile conditions to subside before taking a position.

4th COIN / CANDLE: -
Expect a probable loss for this trade.

3rd COIN / CANDLE: +
Expect a probable loss for this trade.

2nd COIN / CANDLE: -
Expect a probable loss for this trade.

1st COIN / CANDLE: -
Wait for a better opportunity to present itself soon.

PATTERN 40: RELEASE

INTERPRETATION

6th COIN / CANDLE: -
Your profit probabilities are higher with recovery stocks.

5th COIN / CANDLE: -
You will do well in this trade.

4th COIN / CANDLE: +
Ask the advice of your stock broker / advisor before you trade this stock.

3rd COIN / CANDLE: -
Have a stop loss for this trade so that you will be stopped out if there is a price reversal.

2nd COIN / CANDLE: +
You will do very well in this trade.

1st COIN / CANDLE: -
You will do well in this trade.

PATTERN 41: LOSS

INTERPRETATION

6th COIN / CANDLE: +

You will do well in this trade with proper money management.

5th COIN / CANDLE: -

You will do well in this trade.

4th COIN / CANDLE: -

Close your unprofitable positions, if any, before taking fresh positions in any stock.

3rd COIN / CANDLE: -

Trust your judgment on this stock.

2nd COIN / CANDLE: +

You will have to hold on this stock for a while.

1st COIN / CANDLE: +

Don't anticipate huge gains. Exit as soon as your trade is profitable.

PATTERN 42: GAIN

INTERPRETATION

6th COIN / CANDLE: +
This stock is influenced by high frequency traders.

5th COIN / CANDLE: +
You will do well in this trade.

4th COIN / CANDLE: -
If your stock is showing a definitive trend then take a position.

3rd COIN / CANDLE: -
You will do well in this trade.

2nd COIN / CANDLE: -
You will do very well in this trade.

1st COIN / CANDLE: +
You will do very well in this trade.

PATTERN 43: RESOLUTION

INTERPRETATION

6ᵗʰ COIN / CANDLE: -
There is a probability of a sudden price reversal after you take a position in this stock.

5ᵗʰ COIN / CANDLE: +
Don't anticipate huge gains. Exit as soon as your trade is profitable.

4ᵗʰ COIN / CANDLE: +
Expect a probable loss for this trade.

3ʳᵈ COIN / CANDLE: +
There is a probability of sudden price swings after you take a position in this stock.

2ⁿᵈ COIN / CANDLE: +
Expect mixed results with this stock.

1ˢᵗ COIN / CANDLE: +
In spite of your confidence about this stock, expect a probable loss for this trade.

PATTERN 44: CONTACT

INTERPRETATION

6ᵗʰ COIN / CANDLE: +

This stock will soon reach price exhaustion and start falling.

5ᵗʰ COIN / CANDLE: +

Your profit probabilities are higher with undervalued stocks.

4ᵗʰ COIN / CANDLE: +

The entry price which you have planned for this stock is probably high.

3ʳᵈ COIN / CANDLE: +

Expect a probable loss for this trade.

2ⁿᵈ COIN / CANDLE: +

This stock will be whipsawed by high frequency trading. You will find it difficult to take profitable positions.

1ˢᵗ COIN / CANDLE: -

Don't plan a fixed exit point for this stock. Exit as soon as your position is profitable.

PATTERN 45: GATHERING TOGETHER

INTERPRETATION

6th COIN / CANDLE: -

Choose a better stock than this one.

5th COIN / CANDLE: +

Your profit probabilities are higher with leading stocks/ market favorites.

4th COIN / CANDLE: +

You will do very well in this trade.

3rd COIN / CANDLE: -

Limit your position in this stock. Trade up after watching the price action.

2nd COIN / CANDLE: -

You will do very well in this trade.

1st COIN / CANDLE: -

You will find it difficult to exit your position due to the stock's volatility.

PATTERN 46: ASCENDING

INTERPRETATION

6ᵗʰ COIN / CANDLE: -
Expect mixed results with this stock.

5ᵗʰ COIN / CANDLE: -
Limit your initial position in this stock. Trade up after watching the price action.

4ᵗʰ COIN / CANDLE: -
Your profit probabilities are higher with leading stocks.

3ʳᵈ COIN / CANDLE: +
You will do very well in this trade.

2ⁿᵈ COIN / CANDLE: +
You will do very well in this trade.

1ˢᵗ COIN / CANDLE: -
You will do very well in this trade.

PATTERN 47: ADVERSITY

INTERPRETATION

6th COIN / CANDLE: -

Choose a better stock than this one.

5th COIN / CANDLE: +

Expect a probable loss for this trade.

4th COIN / CANDLE: +

You will have to hold on this stock for a while.

3rd COIN / CANDLE: -

Expect a probable loss for this trade.

2nd COIN / CANDLE: +

Wait, if the market appears to be in an over-bought situation.

1st COIN / CANDLE: -

This stock will have few takers when you want to exit.

PATTERN 48: THE WELL

INTERPRETATION

6th COIN / CANDLE: -
You will do very well in this trade.

5th COIN / CANDLE: +
You will do very well in this trade.

4th COIN / CANDLE: -
Your profit probabilities are higher with turnaround/ restructured stocks.

3rd COIN / CANDLE: +
Your profit probabilities are higher with turnaround/ restructured stocks.

2nd COIN / CANDLE: +
Choose a better stock than this one.

1st COIN / CANDLE: -
Stay away from falling/ unknown/ under-performing or thinly traded stocks.

PATTERN 49: CHANGE

INTERPRETATION

6th COIN / CANDLE: -

Wait for present conditions/ trend to change before taking a position.

5th COIN / CANDLE: +

If your stock is showing a definitive trend then take a position.

4th COIN / CANDLE: +

Trade in stocks of companies which have made changes in their top management.

3rd COIN / CANDLE: +

Expect a probable loss for this trade.

2nd COIN / CANDLE: -

If your stock is showing a definitive trend then take a position.

1st COIN / CANDLE: +

Choose a better stock than this one.

PATTERN 50: THE CAULDRON

INTERPRETATION

6th COIN / CANDLE: +

You will do very well in this trade.

5th COIN / CANDLE: -

You will do very well in this trade. Be patient.

4th COIN / CANDLE: +

Expect a probable loss for this trade.

3rd COIN / CANDLE: +

After initial setback, the price of your stock will recover.

2nd COIN / CANDLE: +

If you exit at the right moment then you will make a profit.

1st COIN / CANDLE: -

Close your unprofitable positions, if any, before taking fresh positions in any stock.

PATTERN 51: THUNDER

INTERPRETATION

6th COIN / CANDLE: -

Wait for present conditions/ trend to change before taking a position.

5th COIN / CANDLE: -

Wait for volatile conditions to subside before taking a position.

4th COIN / CANDLE: +

Your stock's trend is not clear at the moment. Choose another stock.

3rd COIN / CANDLE: -

Wait for volatile conditions to subside before taking a position.

2nd COIN / CANDLE: -

The price of your stock will recover after seven days.

1st COIN / CANDLE: +

You will do very well in this trade.

PATTERN 52: KEEPING STILL

INTERPRETATION

6th COIN / CANDLE: +

You will do very well in this trade.

5th COIN / CANDLE: -

If your stock is showing a definitive trend then take a position.

4th COIN / CANDLE: -

Expect a probable loss for this trade.

3rd COIN / CANDLE: +

Expect a probable loss for this trade.

2nd COIN / CANDLE: -

Expect a probable loss for this trade.

1st COIN / CANDLE: -

You will have to hold on this stock for a while.

PATTERN 53: GRADUAL PROGRESS

INTERPRETATION

6th COIN / CANDLE: +

You will do very well in this trade.

5th COIN / CANDLE: +

You will do very well in this trade.

4th COIN / CANDLE: -

Expect mixed results with this stock.

3rd COIN / CANDLE: +

Close your unprofitable positions, if any, before taking fresh positions in any stock.

2nd COIN / CANDLE: -

You will do very well in this trade.

1st COIN / CANDLE: -

Stay away from volatile stocks or stocks of newer companies.

PATTERN 54: THE MARRIAGEABLE MAIDEN

INTERPRETATION

6th COIN / CANDLE: -

Wait. Though this stock looks attractive, it might not prove profitable.

5th COIN / CANDLE: -

If your stock is showing a definitive trend then take a position.

4th COIN / CANDLE: +

Wait for a better opportunity to present itself.

3rd COIN / CANDLE: -

Don't expect much from this stock.

2nd COIN / CANDLE: +

Profits, if any, will not be as per your expectation.

1st COIN / CANDLE: +

You will do very well in this trade.

PATTERN 55: ABUNDANCE

INTERPRETATION

6th COIN / CANDLE: -
Wait for a better opportunity to present itself soon.

5th COIN / CANDLE: -
You will do well in this trade.

4th COIN / CANDLE: +
Trade in trending stocks favored by analysts and institutional investors.

3rd COIN / CANDLE: +
Expect a probable loss for this trade.

2nd COIN / CANDLE: -
Expect a probable loss for this trade.

1st COIN / CANDLE: +
Exit within ten days of taking a position.

PATTERN 56: THE TRAVELLER

INTERPRETATION

6th COIN / CANDLE: +

There might be a slip up while conveying your order to your broker or the broker misinterpreting your instructions for this trade.

5th COIN / CANDLE: -

Please ask your broker to strictly follow your instructions for this trade.

4th COIN / CANDLE: +

Profits, if any, will not be as per your expectation.

3rd COIN / CANDLE: +

Expect a probable loss for this trade.

2nd COIN / CANDLE: -

You will do well in this trade.

1st COIN / CANDLE: -

Expect a probable loss for this trade.

PATTERN 57: THE GENTLE

INTERPRETATION

6ᵗʰ COIN / CANDLE: +

If your stock is showing a definitive trend then take a position. Stay with the trend.

5ᵗʰ COIN / CANDLE: +

This stock will be in the setback stage for three days and then recover for three days.

4ᵗʰ COIN / CANDLE: -

You will do well in this trade.

3ʳᵈ COIN / CANDLE: +

If you have made losses in this stock in the past, then expect a probable loss again.

2ⁿᵈ COIN / CANDLE: +

Don't trade on tips and rumors.

1ˢᵗ COIN / CANDLE: -

Don't over leverage your position in this stock. Limit your position.

PATTERN 58: JOY

INTERPRETATION

6th COIN / CANDLE: -

Is there a possibility of receiving additional benefits from this stock like dividends, stock-splits, buyouts? Investigate.

5th COIN / CANDLE: +

The price of this stock might decline soon.

4th COIN / CANDLE: +

Don't plan a fixed exit point for this stock. Exit as soon as your trade is profitable.

3rd COIN / CANDLE: -

Expect mixed results with this stock.

2nd COIN / CANDLE: +

You will do well in this trade.

1st COIN / CANDLE: +

You will do well in this trade.

PATTERN 59: SCATTERING

INTERPRETATION

6th COIN / CANDLE: +

Choose a better stock than this one.

5th COIN / CANDLE: +

Is there a possibility of receiving additional benefits from this stock like dividends, stock-splits, buyouts? Investigate.

4th COIN / CANDLE: -

Follow the herd.

3rd COIN / CANDLE: -

Profits, if any, will not be as per your expectation.

2nd COIN / CANDLE: +

You will be fooled by false triggers for this stock. Plan your entry/exit points for this trade. Use stop loss.

1st COIN / CANDLE: -

Your profit probabilities are higher with high volume stocks.

PATTERN 60: RESTRAINT

INTERPRETATION

6th COIN / CANDLE: -
After initial setback, the price of your stock will recover.

5th COIN / CANDLE: +
If your stock is showing a definitive trend then take a position.

4th COIN / CANDLE: -
Profits, if any, will not be as per your expectation.

3rd COIN / CANDLE: -
Profits, if any, will not be as per your expectation.

2nd COIN / CANDLE: +
Wait for a better opportunity to present itself soon.

1st COIN / CANDLE: +
Choose familiar stocks. Stay away from unknown/ thinly traded or unfamiliar stocks.

PATTERN 61: INNER SINCERITY

INTERPRETATION

6th COIN / CANDLE: +
Expect a probable loss for this trade.

5th COIN / CANDLE: +
Trust your judgment on this stock.

4th COIN / CANDLE: -
Profits, if any, will not be as per your expectation.

3rd COIN / CANDLE: -
Expect a probable loss for this trade.

2nd COIN / CANDLE: +
You will do well in this trade.

1st COIN / CANDLE: +
You will do well in this trade. Avoid over-hyped stocks.

PATTERN 62: THE SMALL GET BY

INTERPRETATION

6th COIN / CANDLE: -

Your stock is not attractive at this price. You might have missed an opportunity, earlier.

5th COIN / CANDLE: -

Your stock is not attractive at this price.

4th COIN / CANDLE: +

Wait for volatile conditions to subside before taking a position.

3rd COIN / CANDLE: +

Plan your entry/exit points for this trade. Use stop loss.

2nd COIN / CANDLE: -

Expect mixed results with this stock.

1st COIN / CANDLE: -

Your stock is not attractive at this price.

PATTERN 63: AFTER COMPLETION

INTERPRETATION

6th COIN / CANDLE: -

After a severe initial setback, the price of your stock will recover.

5th COIN / CANDLE: +

Stocks of companies situated in the west will do well.

4th COIN / CANDLE: -

Expect mixed results with this stock.

3rd COIN / CANDLE: +

If the market is bearish then wait.

2nd COIN / CANDLE: -

Today's trade may turn profitable in a week's time.

1st COIN / CANDLE: +

You might be stopped out or you will exit in panic. Be patient. Have a contingency plan.

PATTERN 64: BEFORE COMPLETION

INTERPRETATION

6th COIN / CANDLE: +
Limit your position. Exit as soon as your trade turns profitable.

5th COIN / CANDLE: -
You will do well in this trade.

4th COIN / CANDLE: +
You will do well in this trade.

3rd COIN / CANDLE: -
Your profit probabilities are higher with overseas stocks.

2nd COIN / CANDLE: +
You will do well in this trade.

1st COIN / CANDLE: -
Expect a probable loss for this trade.

THANK YOU!

Word-of-mouth publicity is crucial for any author to succeed. If you enjoyed the book, please spread the word and leave a review on Amazon. I would appreciate just a sentence or two.

Please leave your review here http://ASIN.cc/bxxqcL

Thanks for any help you can provide to get the word out!

9 798722 630650